The Accountability Conversation Habit

Becoming Powerful in Difficult Conversations

Quinn Price

The Accountability Conversation Habit

Becoming Powerful in Difficult Conversations

Table of Contents

Introduction

Difficult conversations come in many forms. Anytime someone breaks a commitment, behaves badly, reacts emotionally, or simply isn't meeting your expectations, you have a potentially difficult conversation on your hands.

Will you speak up? And if you do, will you do it in a way that influences the behavior of others while enhancing the relationship? It is possible. In fact, a productive response can become your habitual, instinctive response.

Most people do all they can to avoid confronting the perpetrator. Others overreact, making positive influence nearly impossible as they attempt to force the way on others.

I observed a conversation master while doing a study on high-performing supervisors. When a missed expectation became apparent, the supervisor paused, did a little self-reflection, and then spoke up with respectful candor, curious to understand the gap from the perspective of the violator's viewpoint. Behavior changed, and the relationship was enhanced. He naturally and habitually did something that most people struggle with.

Accountability conversation masters develop a learned *habit* for engaging in productive conversations. I started experimenting with ways of instilling the training and habit in others. It can be learned.

Anyone can create a habit of respectful candor when a gap arises. Not only do I share what to say when others violate an expectation, commitment or behavior, but also how to make the productive reaction your natural response.

We become powerful when we habitually, naturally, and more often than not, behave in ways that influence the behavior of others, while at the same time enhancing a relationship.

We engage in accountability conversations to create change, to influence behavior positively, and to seek both our goals and their needs and goals. Don't miss this point. If we care only about our goals, we tend to manipulate or attempt to overpower the other person. If it's only about their goals, we tend to show up weak, acquiescing to get along rather than engage with care, real power, and influence. Sound familiar?

What do highly-effective hostage negotiators, crisis intervention counselors, effective parents, school leaders and great managers have in common? They approach difficult conversations with deep care for the goals and well-being of others AND are firm about their own goals, ground rules, and options. They approach difficult situations with curiosity, respect, and firmness. They get results that work for all involved within the constraints each situation presents. It's win-win in action.

Real influence, true power in accountability conversations, depends on one's ability to understand and advance the goals of others. Reconciling conflicts, negotiating, de-escalating emotions, helping others make and keep commitments influences behavior to adopt positive change. That's real influence in action.

The promise of this book is not that you'll have the perfect phrases for every situation where an accountability conversation needs to take place. You will have an idea of what to say. You'll know how to say it. But much more importantly, you will develop the *habit* of managing your emotions while being clear about what you want. You will keep the lines of communication open as you seek win-win, shared outcomes that honor the real boundaries each situation presents.

What is the payoff? On a personal level, you gain greater power to influence others in a way that helps them change while improving the relationship. As your skill increases, so does your self-respect. You begin to see opportunity in conflict rather than walls.

At the broader organizational level, a pattern of healthy accountability conversations have proven to be a more powerful predictor of organization success than organization design or other expensive interventions. In other words, culture eats organization design for breakfast. A study published in the Harvard Business Review showed that organization design mattered much less than the pattern of accountability in the organization. The authors set out to show the superiority of process-centered organizations only to find that strong accountability patterns made the organization design work.

The secret sauce of the accountability conversation habit starts with what we call "the golden minute." Mastering one minute makes the difference between effective conversations and poor results. Master the golden minute and you have won 80% of the battle.

Chapter One: Master the Golden Minute

Difficult conversations start long before the words come out of your mouth to the person who disappointed you, let you down, or isn't meeting expectations. They start when you notice the gap, decide if you are going to speak up, and get yourself ready.

Sometimes our mental actions for preparing to speak get derailed by our emotions. We get angry when we notice a problem but don't speak up. We stew over the event, attribute all kinds of evil motives to the person who didn't even bother to read the whole email and do what you asked them to do! Our minds are good at making a mountain out of molehill.

I call the one minute between noticing and speaking up the golden minute because you dramatically increase your chance of success by positively influencing behavior while building the relationship. More of your success comes from the ability to stay calm, curious, and clear about your goal while engaging the other person with respect and firmness.

This chapter gives you an overview of the golden minute while later chapters help you master that minute and what comes after it.

Let's see what's included in the golden minute.

The Golden Minute for Difficult Conversations

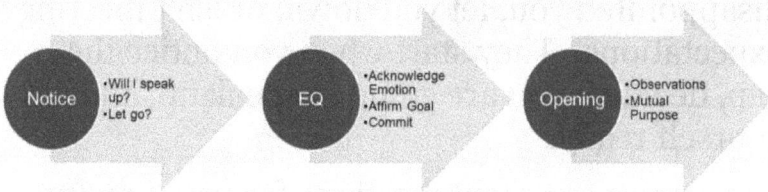

Notice — •Will I speak up? •Let go?

EQ — •Acknowledge Emotion •Affirm Goal •Commit

Opening — •Observations •Mutual Purpose

From Trigger to Decision

The trigger starts when we notice a let down, disappointment, or see bad behavior. This triggers an emotional reaction to the percieved gap.

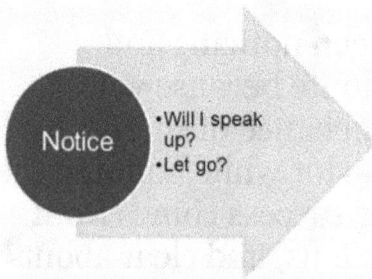

Notice — •Will I speak up? •Let go?

Follow the trigger with a decision. What is the payoff for speaking up or staying silent? Decide if it's worth it or let it go. Train yourself to decide quickly to speak up or not. If you decide to stay silent, let it go. Give yourself some peace.

I stood in line at a famous doughnut place in Portland. The line wound around the block. Yet here we were, waiting for Portland's finest fried bread, when four young men cut in line right in front of us. My eyebrows raised and I sensed disrespect as I considered what they had just done. Is it worth the risk to speak up?

I did, mainly because my companion reminded me that I was the accountability conversation master and could confront anyone. Ego is not a good reason to engage. Yet I did. And I didn't get in a fight. I got calm, then asked them if they knew the line started back there. They huffed, then stepped out of line and headed to the back of the line. My friend saw a calm confrontation in action.

Yet in hindsight, was a doughnut delay worth the risk? In hindsight, the risk wasn't worth the gain.

Consider another situation. A team member missed our team meeting...again. He attended the first fifteen minutes, and then he bolted for the door saying he had another commitment. I fumed. I stewed. How dare he disrespect me and the team this way!

I sent an email reminding everyone on the team how important our team meeting is and thought I had solved the problem.

It happened again. This time he didn't show up, nor did he let me know he had a conflict.

I had delayed the conversation long enough. My silence had cost me a few sleepless nights, angry emotions, and even considered leaving the team for another opportunity. Oh, and somewhere in there I had mentally beat him up and fired him. So goes our emotional life.

Fortunately when I did talk to him, I approached with curiosity to understand his behavior, help him understand my goals, and learn more about his goals. I hoped this would open us to options. I called him to account for his behavior, not with condemnation, accusation, labels, or anger, but with curiosity, respect, and firmness around my goals.

But how much easier would that conversation had been had I decided on the spot to speak to him? What if I was prepared to do so with calm, respect, curiosity, and a fact-based approach?

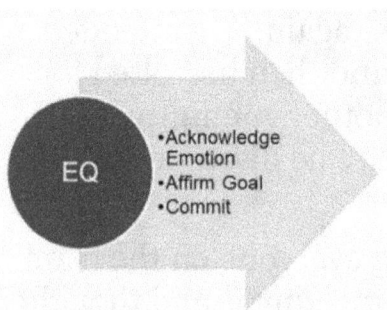

EQ
- Acknowledge Emotion
- Affirm Goal
- Commit

Calm and Clear? EQ in Action

You are on the hostage negotiation team trying to influence David Koresh and his followers, in Waco, Texas. The raid started badly with people on both sides killed. The FBI is not going away. Your goal is getting the hostages out so the dispute with the Branch Davidians can be resolved peacefully.

Gary Noesner writes that one of the most important keys to success was staying calm and focused when others were emotionally triggered. Calm? Yes, Noesner, an expert hostage negotiator knows that an emotionally-flooded brain sees few options and tends to rely on force to resolve complex situations. His "one minute" of power in this difficult influence opportunity started with himself. And this is true for you as well.

Noesner also knew that he needed an open line of communication to influence. Anger and disrespect close that line faster than anything else. Yes, respect is essential to keep the lines of communication open so you can influence the other person while improving the relationship.

Our difficult conversations come in less dramatic opportunities but carry the same dynamic of high emotions and risk.

Perhaps your daughter arrived much later than promised; a team member missed yet another deadline; your boss seems disinterested in knowing that a key project is headed off a cliff; or your spouse has once again spent money you agreed should first be discussed.

If you are emotionally-flooded from assumptions about their motives, you give up influence. You have little chance of creating a breakthrough, much less influencing the behavior of the other person.

How do you quiet the emotional part of your brain so your thinking brain can rule? You must do three critical things.

1. Acknowledge
    a. Acknowledge the emotion that's there. Part of acknowledgement is seeing the assumptions or conclusions you are making about the opportunity.
2. Goal
    a. Affirm what you most want in this situation. Include a mindset of curiosity about their view of the situation and what they want.
3. Commit
    a. Choose a course of action in line with what you most want.

While this sounds like a lot to do when your emotional brain is triggered, I'll teach you how to do this in less than 20 seconds *and* make it habit.

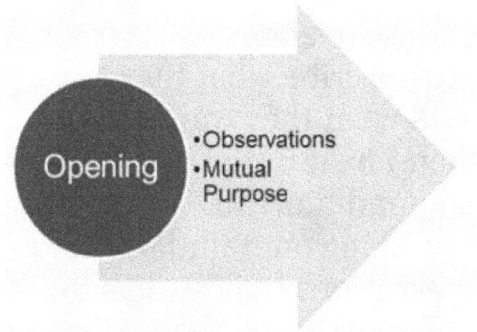

Plan to Open the Conversation

If you are clear about what you want out of the conversation and are calm, respectful and curious, then you are ready to open your mouth in the most productive way possible. This alone won't guarantee success, but will set the tone to improve the likelihood of effective influence.

You must be clear about what you have observed versus what you have decided. Sharing assumptions, conclusions, accusations kill the conversation and create barriers that limit our ability to influence behavior.

Also, know what result you want from speaking up. What do you want to be better? If you're irritated and want the other person to know that, refine your goal. Perhaps you want a better working relationship and just saw something that gets in the way of that goal. Do you see how being clear about a worthy goal makes the opening so much easier?

When I coach people who are about to confront someone, I ask them to describe what they have seen or experienced and what they want out of the conversation. When I hear outcomes that aren't observable and sound more like conclusions, we keep working on it until we find the event, data, or observations that lead us to believe we have a problem

Good accountability conversation openers come in one of three approaches.

The Question and Goal

The question and the goal approach is the simplest of all the openings. It's simply asking them a question to understand more about their current mind-set. Then reiterate your goal. Here's an example.

- "What is your stress level on a scale of 1 to 10? I want to help."

The Observation/ Consequence/ Goal/ Question

Here's an example of what this opening sounds like.

- "I noticed that you left our team meeting 15 minutes into it. I'm concerned because our team time is essential to aligning across projects. I want to understand more about your priorities so we can find a way for you to meet your client needs while aligning with other projects. How does that sound?"

Topic / Contrast / Question

This is a slight variation that contrasts what we want with what we don't want in the conversation.

- "I want to talk to you about your attendance at our team meeting. What I don't want to do is come across as a parent telling you to clean your room, yet I also want to understand what's going on in your world so we can find ways of meeting your client needs and our need to align across different projects. How does that sound?"

This gives you an idea of what is coming as we practice, master and make the critical one minute a habit as we approach difficult conversations.

Should we speak up? If so, get yourself ready to speak up with the best possible opening to meet the goal of influencing behavior while improving the relationship. Once you learn to do this as a habit, you'll wonder why it was ever a big deal to talk to someone about a gap, an issue, a problem, or their behavior.

Chapter Two: Get Calm and Clear in 20 Seconds or Less

Anytime we believe that we're being...

- Disrespected

- Treated unfairly

- Under appreciated

- Ignored or misunderstood

- Held to unrealistic deadlines

...our emotional brain signals a fear response (freezing, fight, flight, or fear) that produces poor conversations and reduces them to rubble. Can you think of a time when your first response, especially an angry response, got the best results in influencing the behavior of another?

Imagine someone assumes the worst about you and begins an accountability conversation with anger-based labels and accusations like...

- "You are a loser!" Or, "I'm not sure I want to work with you anymore, with the deadlines you've missed lately". And, like

I've heard from others, "You're just not someone who delivers".

- "You just don't love me anymore. Don't try to deny it! I don't even know why you married me. Why should I stay with you?"

- "You're underperforming. I think you should be fired. A key client you work with said so. Well, how are you going to get your performance back on track?"

Openings like these shut down lines of communication, increase defensiveness, and trigger our emotional brains to close down options. Our emotional brain mobilizes us to freeze, fight, or flee rather than creatively consider options.

The question is, how do I get calm and able to engage others in an effective conversation when anger is my dominant emotion?

In the previous chapter, we must master three actions.

1. Acknowledge
   a. Acknowledge the emotion that's there. Part of acknowledgement is seeing the assumptions or conclusions you are making about the situation.

2. Goal
    a. Affirm what you most want in this situation. Include curiosity about their view of the situation.
3. Commit
    a. Choose a course of action in line with what you most want.

I recently got in an accident. It was a dark and stormy night, poor visibility and a car came out of nowhere, colliding with my car. Talk about emotionally triggered!

As I got out of my car to see how the other person was doing, my heart was racing as other cars stopped to help. I felt frozen, barely able to function. I knew this wasn't a good response given that I needed to manage the situation.

I started to acknowledge what was pulsing through my veins. I acknowledged to myself that I felt frightened, confused, and anxious. Breathe. I didn't bother with assumptions as I knew why I felt this way. I just got in an accident. But what did I most want? To make sure everyone was ok. Then I needed to get eyewitness names and accident pictures in case I would need them. Keeping my emotions calm meant the other driver would get the help they needed and I would have protection from litigation. It took me less than 20 seconds to go from freaked out to competent to act.

 In fact, it turned out that no one had called 911 to report the accident. I did so. I started snapping pictures of the accident scene. The details I noted helped the officer on the scene declare that I was not at fault and he would represent that fact in the report.

I shook slightly from the adrenalin as I drove away but I acted productively despite the overpowering emotion. Am I a superman? No, I am simply someone who has practiced the three steps to the point where my mind and body get what I am doing and quickly align to support me.

Fast-forward to an accountability conversation with a member of my team who had performance issues. He failed to update his weekly report again. I realized I need to speak with him about this and some related issues. I had allowed myself to get busy with a demanding consulting and educational delivery schedule and it showed with this particular team member.

I looked inside to understand my emotions. I noticed irritation bordering anger. Why? Oh, I was assuming bad motives on his part, assuming that he saw how busy I was and was taking advantage of me. I questioned that assumption and felt better immediately.

I was starting to feel curious about what he might be thinking. I thought about what I wanted from the conversation and quickly identified greater consistency on the weekly report and attention to client deadlines as my main goal. I identified when and how to talk to him. I liked this guy and now felt better, more curious, respectful, yet firm that we needed to talk. I was ready.

The conversation went well. I opened with "I want to talk to you about your weekly report, but I don't want to come across as scolding or parental, just trying to understand what's helping you sort through your priorities so we can better align. Does that make sense?"

He walked me into the key priorities that often pushed the weekly report off the plate. I realized that I rarely gave him feedback on his report, giving the impression that I didn't value them. I did, but that's the point of a good accountability conversation; greater understanding and more choices for course correction. I kept the lines of communication open through respect, curiosity, and by asking good questions.

Practice emotional acknowledgement right now. What emotion are you experiencing at the moment? Why? How are your assumptions shaping your emotional life? Acknowledge those assumptions. What do you want most in this moment? What's next?

How long did that take you? Most people I coach report that it takes between 10 to 30 seconds. That's time well invested. All your conversations will be better, especially the difficult conversations about the behavior of another person you want to influence. Start with yourself. Greater emotional maturity leads to higher performance and it leads to much better accountability conversations.

When you are calm, clear about your outcome, and curious to learn more, you are now in the best place to start the conversation. Do this well and you have a greater than 80% chance of a positive outcome that changes behavior and improves a relationship. Do this poorly and you lose influence and may lose the relationship.

Start to develop the habit through practice. When you sense strong emotions surging when life happens, acknowledge what's going on, acknowledge the assumptions that drive the emotion, and then see what you most want to take action to move towards that.

Positive habits develop when we respond intentionally to a trigger rather than let old habits take over. It's especially important that you let yourself link the positive emotions of greater control, greater effectiveness with the trigger and route we described here.

We will work on this habit more in chapter to come. Right now we need to deepen our understanding of how to kick off the conversation in the most productive way.

Chapter Three: Plan the Conversation Opener

I remember the day when a person I respect called and said, in an accusatory voice, "Is it true that you...." and proceeded to share half-truths and accusations that came from a hurt person who had been in my life. I tried not to respond with the same emotion but lay out what had really happened in a calm and caring way.

After I answered his questions with clear and what I thought was compelling evidence, I asked him what he wanted to get out of the conversation. He didn't know other than he said he didn't trust me. Again, I tried not to respond with strong emotions but kept the lines of communication open. I wanted to help him understand what had happened and why from my standpoint.

He never believed me. In fact, the more calm and direct I was, the more agitated he became. He ended the conversation with "You need help!" He was saying that despite what I told him, he didn't trust me and thought I was a damaged individual.

As he hung up, my emotions came with no restraint. I was stunned and angry. My father had died just three days before and I had hoped for a little support rather than these baseless judgments. He had no idea what he wanted out of the conversation. He not only came into the conversation with a loaded emotional agenda, his opening was nothing more than an accusation disguised as a question. He ended it as poorly as he began, with ignorance, unchallenged assumptions, and accusation.

Conversations matter. In many ways, conversations are the relationship.

I never spoke to this man again. A common project we both cared about died that day. You could easily say the relationship died that day as well.

Why all the relationship carnage? I view the cause as unchallenged assumptions, out of control emotions, no curiosity, much animosity, no respect, and a poor opening.

When I teach people how to open an accountability conversation, I give them approaches and phases that work, UNLESS your thinking and heart are still in a toxic place. No words will make up for that. If you're trying to sound curious yet aren't, they will pick that up and respond accordingly.

In Chapter One I shared the general approaches to opening an accountability conversation. Let's dig into each in more depth to understand when and how to use them.

The Question

The easiest opening is a question. In the doughnut line, I simply asked, "Are you aware the line starts over there?" Of course, my voice tone matters a great deal. But assuming I'm respectful and curious, a question is often all that's needed.

A teen had been disrespectful in class. He was sent to the Principal's office. The Principal could have said many things including a lecture on class respect, the history of the school, you name it, yet he simply asked a sincere and probing question.

"What is your current stress level on a scale from 1 to 10? I want to help, not increase it."

That led to a good conversation where the key stress drivers came out and they dealt with the root issues. The teen did not escape punishment yet did feel respected, understood, and that he had an adult in his corner that cared. The teen experienced accountability in a way that included respect and firmness. It changed behavior and improved this young man's life.

The Sweet Spot of the Accountably Mindset

If you believe the path to victory in a difficult situation is force or using your positional power out of the starting gate, you may regret it. The paradox of power is that force has a cost and it comes back to us in ways we might not expect.

Use force as a last resort rather than your influence habit of choice and you'll gain more commitment by keeping the lines of communication open while holding the line of your goals and boundaries.

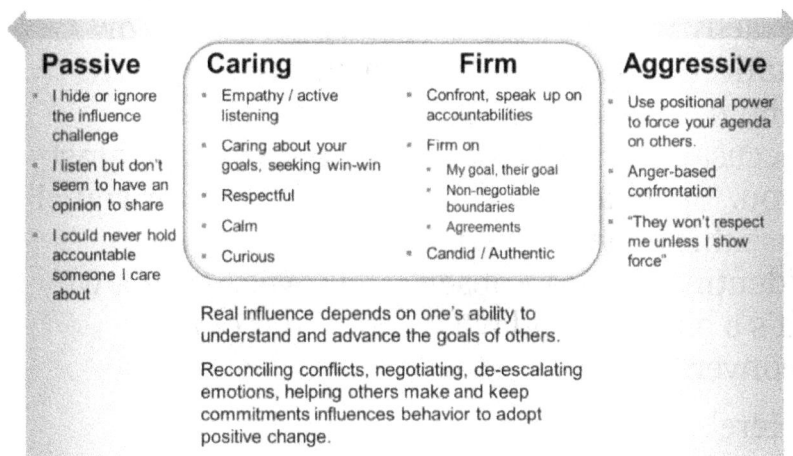

Passive	Caring	Firm	Aggressive
• I hide or ignore the influence challenge	• Empathy / active listening	• Confront, speak up on accountabilities	• Use positional power to force your agenda on others.
• I listen but don't seem to have an opinion to share	• Caring about your goals, seeking win-win	• Firm on	• Anger-based confrontation
• I could never hold accountable someone I care about	• Respectful	• My goal, their goal	• "They won't respect me unless I show force"
	• Calm	• Non-negotiable boundaries	
	• Curious	• Agreements	
		• Candid / Authentic	

Real influence depends on one's ability to understand and advance the goals of others.

Reconciling conflicts, negotiating, de-escalating emotions, helping others make and keep commitments influences behavior to adopt positive change.

An excessively passive approach doesn't work either. Passivity creates an unwritten understanding the behavior of others is acceptable.

The accountability habit starts with a mind-set that real influence depends on your ability to understand and advance the goals of others.

Approaching Others

Use a simple question when you want to know what happening with someone to begin the dialogue.

The Observation / Consequence / Goal / Question

This approach works only if you start by stating exactly what you have seen, experienced, or noticed rather than the conclusions you have about those events. Any personal label, accusation, or blanket statement works against you. Specific, observable events work for you. I use this opening the most as it forces me to identify what I've observed or experienced, why it's a big deal, and what I want out of the conversation.

Here's an example.

"I noticed that you left our team meeting 15 minutes into it." This is what I saw. You're not putting any judgment on this but rather are simply stating what you noticed.

The consequence is stating why you're concerned.

"I'm concerned because our team time is essential to aligning across projects."

If you can't come up with a potential consequence, then perhaps it's not a big deal. Perhaps it's simply your expectations that have been violated. Adjust your expectations and save everyone the drama of a bad conversation.

Next, state why you want to talk about this or the goal of the conversation.

"I want to understand more about your priorities so we can find a way for you to meet your client needs while aligning with other projects."

Great accountability conversations meet your goals and their goals. Therefore, the wording includes both your goal and an opening to learn more about their wants and needs.

Finally, we end with a question. That opens the door to communication, to better understanding of what's going on.

"How does that sound?"

Putting it all together, this approach follows this format.

- I noticed _____ (Specific observations)

- I'm concerned because _____(Consequence)

27

- I want to talk about this because
  _____(Your goal or purpose)

- How should I be thinking about this?
  (Question)

A few cautions are in order. Anytime you open an accountability conversation with more than four sentences, you run the risk of lecturing. Lecturing rarely changes behavior and is often used to get them to recognize what you're feeling rather than solve a problem.

The biggest mistake with this approach is stating a conclusion while pretending it's something you observed. Admittedly this can be tedious if you think you need to share a long list of things you've observed. That makes it sound like you're making a case against the person rather than teeing up a good conversation that will lead to changed behaviors. The solution is to share specific examples to give them an idea of what you're bringing to their attention without giving them the whole list.

Topic / Contrast / Question

The third approach sets the agenda while setting up an expectation for the conversation of what you do want to talk about and the impressions you don't want to give.

Here's an example.

"I want to talk to you about your attendance at our team meeting. What I don't want to do is come across as a parent telling you to clean your room. Yet I want to understand what's going on in your world so we can find ways of meeting your client needs and our need to align across different projects. How does that sound?"

I use this approach when the topic is personally sensitive or I suspect that respect might be at risk out of the gate. This helps to assure them that I want to preserve respect while discussing a difficult topic.

Summary

There are three main openings to an accountability conversation that work well. One is a simple question. The second choice or the main approach includes what we've noticed, why it's important, the goal of the conversation and a transitional question. Finally, we saw how

29

contrast statements can be woven in to help keep safe boundaries in the conversation.

Before we learn how to navigate the rest of the accountability conversation, let's dig into the golden moment, deepening the critical habit that makes such a difference in creating positive outcomes.

The Golden Minute for Difficult Conversations

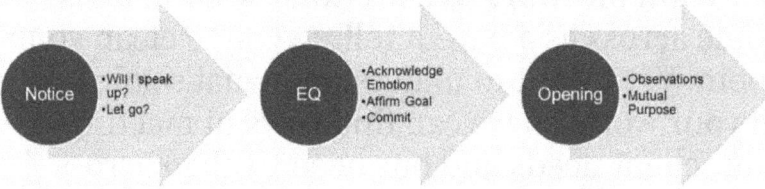

Notice
- Will I speak up?
- Let go?

EQ
- Acknowledge Emotion
- Affirm Goal
- Commit

Opening
- Observations
- Mutual Purpose

Chapter Four: Create the Golden Minute Habit

Chapters Five and beyond teach you how to respond to issues once the accountability conversation is in motion. You'll learn how to break through conversation quicksand through all the predictable issues that come up.

But having worked with many people in creating accountability conversation excellence, mastery of the golden minute produces 80% of the results from great conversations. When we go in with the right mind-set and are intent, calm and clear, we set a tone that influences other people. The habit of accountability conversation preparation will reward you with self-respect, power, and the satisfaction of getting results by influencing the behavior of others.

How do we create a habit?

First, let's define what a habit is. It is an *instinctual response to a trigger*. A habit is sustained by an *anticipation of a reward*.

Emergency workers and military personnel create habits to respond productively when the fur and bullets are flying. They are trained to instinctively react regardless of what else may be going on. Their lives depend on it.

Training these instinctual responses or habits requires three critical elements:

- The trigger or beginning event. It's the "when" that starts a productive response.

- A process, routine or set of behaviors you do without thinking or the "what."

- A reward or payoff for engaging in the behaviors.

Our brains are wired to support us surviving, getting more pleasure, and avoiding pain. Research confirms that abundant situational practice with clear triggers (when) and the expectation of a reward linked to the behavior sets up a habit.

Identify Triggers

Triggers for accountability conversations show up in endless variations given that you never know when someone will misbehave. Yet I ask you right now to identify as many typical situations where you are likely to notice the potential need to have an accountability conversation.

Identify Your Natural Emotional Reaction

For each of the triggers or situations you identified, what would you first feel? What normally happens in your body when you notice a gap, issue, missed expectation, or broken promise?

Imagine the Reward

Assume for a moment that you decide to talk to the person and it goes well. How would that feel?

Have you ever had an accountability conversation and experienced a reward or payoff for doing so? Think back to a time when you had an accountability conversation, spoke up when something wasn't right, and you felt an emotional payoff for doing so. Allow yourself to reexperience that right now.

When I ask people to describe the payoff they get when they speak up in the face of bad behavior, I hear rewards like

- Increased self-respect
- Sense that I helped to solve a problem while building a relationship
- I made a difference
- I feel more powerful

Zero in on a reward you have or could experience because of engaging in an accountability conversation.

Now allow your body to experience that emotion as if you had just completed a great accountability conversation. What are you hearing? How would your shoulders feel during this moment of self-respect, sense of accomplishment, or increased personal power? Imagine the reward moment as clearly as you can.

As you imagine this, say to yourself, "I spoke up with integrity, care and with their best interest at heart. I respect myself." Repeat this as you imagine the conversation going well. Remind yourself that you got here by speaking up with respect and seeking to create common purpose.

Envisioning the Response

Go back to a situation you identified. You notice a problem; feel a pit in your stomach. Now identify the most productive response to the situation and emotion, a response that would bring you to the reward you just imagined.

For me I imagined my one-on-one meetings where I often found out about a gap or issue, then imagined my first emotional reaction, then getting calm, focused, and engaging them in problem solving.

See yourself deciding to speak up, getting calm, respectful, curious and planning to speak up in a way that sets the right tone.

Allow your body to fully experience the positive emotions of seeing a gap, approaching it with curiosity, and engaging with the person to find the best solutions.

Again, imagine the positive result, then walk through the trigger, your first emotional reaction, all leading up to the payoff of speaking up with integrity.

Mental rehearsal is how top organizations create productive habits with customer service representatives who face angry customers, soldiers in battle, or emergency workers navigating horrific conditions.

Find someone to role play with you. Practice is essential to building the habit of a productive golden minute.

In addition to practice, find situations where it's wise to speak up. Practice the golden minute. I'm not asking you to confront every situation but to use your golden minute to decide, and then act based on that decision. Let go if you choose not to engage.

Once we're in a good accountability conversation, how do we navigate it? Where do these conversations derail and what do we do?

Chapter Five:
Analyze the Causes

Most productive accountability conversations include questions to identify causes of the current behavior and find choices for action.

Why do people do what they do? If our answer includes evil motives such as making our lives a living hell, then you won't have much influence with the person you are engaging in an accountability conversation. Assuming bad motives will lead to anger which in turn leads to poor lines of communication which results in low influence, damaged relationships, and poor results.

Behavior is much more complex. We often have many reasons or drivers of behavior, many of which we find hard to articulate even when we are the ones doing the behaviors! One sure killer of productive accountability conversations are glib assumptions about WHY someone is behaving as they are. Eat a little humble pie and acknowledge that you don't know and need to find out by getting curious and asking many questions.

I know I am likely to sustain the desired behavior if the elements of the acronym "CLEAR" are present. If someone is committed, aware of leverage factors that drive habits (trigger, response, and payoff), have the right expectations, is able, and is reinforced for it, we're likely to sustain the behavior.

CLEAR Element	Internal (Me)	Factors Outside of Me
Commitment	I have a strong why (based on pain or compelling future)	Others coach me to motivate and paint a picture of compelling future
	I am aware of the need to change or do new behaviors	Others coach me on how I interpret my current reality
	I've made a committed decision	I went public with my commitment decision
	I know what my next steps are	Others are holding me accountable for actions I'm committed to
	I'm acting on my next steps	

CLEAR Element	Internal (Me)	Factors Outside of Me
Leverage	There's a clear trigger - It might be a visual cue, a sound, smell, location, time, a person, your emotional state, and body sensations at the time, anything that precedes your response or action. I respond with the new behaviors And there's a payoff that I find pleasurable	I see reminders that lead me to act on my commitments. It's relatively easy or convenient to act on my commitments I don't want to let down people I respect so I keep my commitments

CLEAR Element	Internal (Me)	Factors Outside of Me
Expectations	I believe the habit or new normal is possible and probable; or I believe I have or am the new normal, just not yet displayed physically I see the habit or new normal as an extension of who I am	Others influence me about what is acceptable, permissible, expected, and what events mean that align with bringing out the new normal
Ability	I can do the new behaviors well (I've practiced, I have good role models, I've been mentored, I am at mastery level)	Others enable me through feedback, reminding me, mentoring, coaching, modeling, providing time for me to practice

CLEAR Element	Internal (Me)	Factors Outside of Me
Reinforcement	With the new normal, I get a personal payoff I find meaningful (see Leverage)	Others encourage the new normal through feedback, affirmation, reward, and other positive forms of support

I use CLEAR in three ways.

1- Humility; to humbly realize that behavior is influenced by many factors and I need to understand them all. That realization helps me get curious, and I've never regretted curiosity in approaching someone with the attitude of wanting to learn more.

2- CLEAR moves me away from assuming evil motives to considering other reasons that influence behavior. I need to understand all factors that cause poor performance or the gap I'm seeing. The elements of CLEAR provide an approach to identify the issues that most affect behavior.

3- Use CLEAR to get results. CLEAR provides guidance in exploring choices for improving behavior.

Use CLEAR as a way to find out what is influencing the behavior you don't want or what might help to motivate the desired behavior.

Once you start an accountability conversation, move into analysis mode to understand what, from their perspective, is driving or influencing the behavior you noticed, and what choices are available to reinforce new behaviors. Become a student of what influences behavior. This will help you becomes less of a judge and more of a coach.

This became clearer to me when I was trying to influence the behavior of an emotionally explosive child of mine. Let's just say his impulses were on overdrive. Yet a wise coach told me to treat his behavior as an ability problem, not motivation. He helped me coach my son to slow down his impulsive responses and allow his thinking brain to catch up to the emotional brain. I got calmer and more powerful while my son increased his ability to manage his behavior. Our "accountability conversations" became much more an opportunity to coach him on his reactions rather try to "amp up" the motivation.

When I'm curious about what is driving behavior, not assuming the worst or assuming evil motives, I'm in a much stronger position to influence their behavior. That, of course, is the point of an effective accountability conversation.

Analysis leads to creating a commitment. Strong commitments provide the foundation for future accountability conversations as you increase your ability to influence the behavior of others with care and firmness. How do we get commitment? And how do we make a habit out of effective commitment conversations?

Chapter Six: The Secret of Creating Commitment

I thought I had a solid commitment after a good accountability conversation with a certain team member. The issue was letting other team members know where she was so we could better coordinate team activities. She agreed. Problem solved.

But then it happened again. Back we went into the accountability conversation. Again I got a commitment. When it happened again, we ended up in another accountability conversation.

Why did we keep coming back to the same issue?

When we do superficial analysis, we miss the real causes and effective fixes. Analysis matters and investing in deeper cause exploration often pays off with better commitments.

I've found that when I'm vague in the commitment part of the conversation, I set myself up for a repeat. That was the case of the missing team member. I simply wasn't effective in my commitment-making habits.

What is the secret to a good commitment conversation?

First, be clear who is going to do what by when. Most of us do that. Now take your commitments to the next level by doing the following five crucial behaviors to cement next-step actions:

1- Reconnect the commitment actions to the original goal.

   - "So to make our team align better on our critical goals, I'm agreeing to _____ and you agree to _____.

2- Clarify how will we judge "goodness" or "how well" behavior meets expectations

   - "We'll know we're hitting this mark if we _____."

3- Clarify the boundaries or conditions that need to be honored

   - "I see us doing location updates twice a day. Agree?"

4- Identify feedback and follow up mechanisms

   - "Let's review how this is going in our next one on one. Also, I'd like you to reach out to other team members to get their read on this new approach."

5- Identify your immediate next action

- "So, our immediate next step is to
_____."

When I add in these five crucial behaviors, I end up with strong commitments that create strong momentum for sustainable behaviors.

Creating the Commitment Conversation Habit

Do the following to create a commitment conversation habit:

- ☐ I get motivated by remembering how painful silence can be. I want to get the commitment right the first time.

- ☐ I imagine a great-feeling end result; I had a good commitment conversation and it felt great.

- ☐ I imagine the trigger or initiative event for the commitment conversation.

- ☐ I imagine the steps above to get crystal clear about the "who does what by when" issues and how we're going to follow up without it feeling like overkill.

☐ I allow myself to feel the payoff of being crystal clear.

As one person in a seminar I conducted said, "If I would have done the commitment conversation well up front, the accountability part wouldn't be as necessary."

And when you're in a tough conversation, how do you navigate the "unaccountable" mind-sets that seem so plentiful today?

Chapter Seven: Navigate Low Accountability Reactions

People have developed many anti-accountability routines. Once you know how to productively navigate them, you dramatically increase your ability to influence behavior.

The passively unaccountable use unproductive solutions such as:

- The Vacationer. They view their accountabilities as icing on the cake; if they ignore or underperform a duty, they can't be held accountable because since they don't own it.

- The Victim. Nothing is their fault. They deny the issue, diminish the consequences, and deflect responsibility to others.

- Hiding. They avoid personal visibility because it might be scrutinized. They often try to change the topic or make it about you to shift focus away from them.

- Waiting Game. They avoid accountability by deflecting to others for not providing needed inputs or decisions.

The actively unaccountable behaviors show up as follows:

- Not My Job. They own very little and actively make sure they sign up for as little as possible.

- Blame Shifter. They actively shift blame to anyone else, including you when they smell any kind of accountability conversation.

- Legalistic Tail Covering. They engage in endless debate, detailed and extensive emails, all under the guise of avoiding real accountability and confusing the issue.

- Intimidators. They use some form of intimation or force when confronted with an accountability gap.

How do you navigate these forms of low accountability when they come up in the accountability conversation?

What doesn't work is using any of these "low accountability" labels when you see this behavior. That's not the answer and why I don't present these types of low accountability mind-sets too soon. It's not about labeling them but all about how you respond.

The best response is simple so don't write this off too quickly as glib advice.

Know going in to the conversation the following:

- <u>Observations</u>. Share what you've observed or know for sure rather than offering labels or conclusions.

- <u>Goal</u>. State your goal or what you want to make better.

- <u>Consequence</u>. State why it's an issue or the main motive to make an adjustment.

- <u>Calm</u>. Maintain a calm emotional state that keeps you open to many solutions rather than push for one because you are agitated.

Calm, curious, caring and committed to mutual outcomes wins the day. Redirect the conversation when they try a low accountability response by staying focused on the outcome you want and connecting to what they want. Keep the lines of communication open so you can analyze causes and find good solutions.

Example- Not My Fault

Let's assume that a blame shifter/victim has not completed a report by the promised deadline. Notice how the expert handles this.

Manager: I noticed the report you agreed to complete by noon wasn't completed. I'm concerned because we use that information to compile the monthly Officer report. What happened?

Employee: Oh, speaking of Officer, our Marketing Director called and asked for the monthly sales numbers. He seemed pleased that I responded quickly.

Manager: I recognize your responsiveness, and I want to talk about how you manage your commitment deadlines with others on the team. Can we agree that if something comes up that looks like a higher priority, that you let me know?

This example works because the Manager was clear going in that the issue was how the employee made priority choices. The manager used observations rather than conclusions in opening this conversation and moved it back to the main issues she wanted to solve.

Example – Blame Shift

Manager: I noticed that you arrived at your desk at 7:20 when our agreed on start time is 7. What happened?

Employee: Oh, really? Why do you always pick on me! I see other people arriving late all the time and I don't see you calling them out. What is it about me that brings out the police officer in you?

Manager: (Calm, focused, smiling, not taking the bait) We can discuss my job as a supervisor in another conversation, but I want to discuss your arrival today and understand more about what happened.

Employee: Traffic. I mean, traffic sometimes gets to be a challenge.

Manager: I understand. I have traffic challenges myself. But I want to talk about your responsibility to show up on time as it's critical to how our call center operates.

This example works because the Manager stayed calm, didn't take the bait, knew the problem they wanted to solve and stayed with it. You can do the same.

Example – Not My Job

Team Member 1: I noticed that you didn't write up the meeting notes as you've done in the past. I find your notes helpful. What happened?

Team Member 2: Notes, yes like it's my job. Hey I was just trying to help and well, why should I get stuck with this, for jumping in when I did?

<u>Team Member 1</u>: I don't want you to feel like you are stuck with it but I think someone should be taking notes. Would you be okay if I brought this up to the team leader, the need to have someone own team meeting notes?

This example works because the issue is no one owns the team meeting notes. Navigate this by identifying someone to own this and make that ownership clear through a commitment conversation.

Summary

The pattern in all these examples shows the need to do the following:

-   Come into the conversation knowing what you have seen, wanting to meet your goal.

-   Staying calm when they push back.

-   Continuing to be respectful while also being firm about your goals and boundaries.

What doesn't work is to label the individual, get mad, or move too quickly to positional power or force. Remember, you will win if you keep focused on the problem you want to solve, stay calm, and keep the lines of communication open as you explore causes and solutions. Care with firmness wins the day.

But what to you do when the other person gets angry or has an emotional reaction you didn't expect? How do you de-escalate an emotional reaction?

Chapter Eight: De-Escalate Emotional Reactions

Hostage negotiators, crisis intervention counselors, good parents, and effective police officers know something about how to deal with freaked out people. We need to know what they know.

What doesn't work is to order them to calm down. You've done that too? Has it been done to you? And did it work? Most agree that it doesn't.

What does? We've learned some things about our emotional brain and how to manage it. These insights may save your life.

Meet My Emotional Needs and Don't Piss Me Off

Hostage negotiator Gary Noesner entitled his book, "Stalling for Time," because that's what he does; he tries to slow down action and decision making so the person in the crisis can think clearer. Give the emotional brain time to deal with the flood of emotions so the more rational brain can catch up.

But it's more than just slowing things down; it's making sure we meet basic human needs for the following:

- Respect
- To feel understood
- To be treated fairly
- To help them meet their goals

That is why Noesner often starts a hostage negotiation with a statement like "I'm here to help. Help me understand what's going on in there."

Why? To communicate a desire to understand life from their viewpoint so they feel understood, respected and can begin the process of understanding what they want. It's the basis for creating a win-win outcome for all involved.

Remember our High School Principal that was influencing the disrespectful student? He asked a question to understand. Why? Because we all want to feel understood.

What does that mean for you?

Imagine a situation where someone responds with anger or an intense emotion to your conversation. What can you say to help them manage their emotions?

Acknowledge and seek to understand

Here are some examples of what you can say as you calm yourself, stay respectful and focused on the best possible outcome.

"You seem upset about this. Help me understand what's upsetting you."

"What is your current stress level on a scale from 1 to 10? Why? What's driving that?"

"I don't want to upset you and I want to understand more about your situation so we can find a solution that work for both of us."

Containment

I know people who use emotions to manipulate people and get their own way. You feed the manipulation monster when they see their outburst control you. Caring with calm, candor and commitment to mutual purpose shows strength while keeping the lines of communication open.

The FBI starts all hostage negotiation with containment. That lets the perpetrator know that they aren't walking out without consequences. They contain the situation, and then reach out with respect and firm boundaries. Sure, the perpetrator wants the FBI to go away, but they establish a hard boundary that they won't go away.

Our High School Principal sought to understand yet he held firm to consequences. Apply this approach when dealing with bad behavior.

How can you use containment? Stay firm on what you want to solve (your goal or purpose) while also meeting their emotional needs while learning more about what's most important to them.

Here are some examples of how that would play out in an accountability conversation.

"I understand you're upset. I think if we keep the lines of communication open we can find a solution that works for you and meets my needs as well. How does that sound?"

You can acknowledge the emotion, seek to understand more, AND be firm about your goal, real boundaries, and consequences if this is what needs to happen. Never let the emotional reaction of another push you into an emotional response. Once you do, your options shut down and the conversation will unravel.

When It Gets Personal

Sometimes the emotional reaction includes personally disparaging remarks. Acknowledge the emotion and set boundaries. You don't have to put up with personal insults, especially in a business environment.

As an example, imagine that you started a conversation with someone who loves to bring stinky food in for lunch each day. The smell distracts and disgusts you. You approach them in a calm, respectful way, ask to talk about the smell of their lunch choices, and the next thing you know, they are calling you every disparaging name they can think of.

Here's a good reaction to their overreaction.

"You sound upset that I brought this up. I want to understand more about your view of the situation and find a solution that works for everyone AND I won't put up being called a _____. Can you agree to that?"

This works because you acknowledge the emotion, restate the win-win you want to pursue, and set boundaries. Then you ask for agreement on those boundaries. If they continue, you must leave the situation and escalate to managers, law enforcement. Anyone who continues to come at you with violence even after you deal with it respectfully and skillfully has deeper problems. Get to safety.

Summary

How do you de-escalate an emotional reaction? Don't pour gas on the fire by commanding them to calm down or getting upset with them, but in meeting their emotional needs to be understood, respected, be treated fairly, and get their goals met. You can also set firm boundaries to the conversation. They will respect you when you do.

What do we do if they really don't care about solving the problem we seem so set on solving? It's time to bring out the motivation enhancers we learn about in the next chapter.

Chapter Nine: "Amp Up" the Motivation

Occasionally you find that you do everything right; you open the conversation with skill, respect and curiosity, only to see an odd response from the person you want to influence.

They yawn. Or they shrug. They don't care about the issue you're bringing up.

Why? The consequences or goal you mention doesn't resonate with them. Or they're powerful and don't feel the need to address anything from you. Whatever the reason, they simply don't see the benefit to them and don't want to engage in the conversation.

I ran into this with a leader I coached. I brought up a topic that he simply didn't care to discuss. At first I thought his resistance was due to fear but the deeper I dug the more it became clear he simply didn't care how he was affecting a team member.

What can you do when the other person isn't motivated to address the issue you want to address?

I've found four tactics that work. You don't nessissarily need all four but you may need to employ them all from time to time.

1. Help them link the consequences of their actions to what they care about

This sounds easy but the difficult part is knowing enough about their world to know what goals to link to. In the case of the reluctant manager, I linked the team member abuse to the promotion I knew he wanted.

You can use a similar tactic on a teenager. What do they want? Most want more freedom or independence. How would you use a missed curfew, something they don't care about or think is a big deal, with their desire for freedom?

This is what it would sound like.

(Calm, curious, and caring) "I understand that you don't see the reason for making it home when we agreed. But think of it this way. The more trust we build together, the more latitude I can give you, or the more freedom you'll experience. That's why coming home when you agreed to builds trust. When you don't, it works against trust, not to mention I worry. I love you and want to know you're safe. And I want to give you as much freedom as trust will allow."

2. Reveal hidden victims

We often make decisions with little knowledge of who it affects downstream. That's why an effective marketing campaign helped people understand the effect of garbage disposal on aquatic animals. We do the same when we highlight consequences or bring out the victims, so to speak. This more graphically illustrates the impact of their choices downstream or on others.

When a hard-charging manager understood that his style contributed to a recent stress leave taken by a direct report, his motivation to change improved. He decided to learn how to use different styles of leadership to fit the needs of the situation.

3. Hold up a mirror, help them see how others see them (see social consequences)

Executive coaches have done this for a long time. They use surveys, interviews or other forms of feedback to motivate people to change. So can you.

A leader I was coaching seemed barely interested in change until I presented him with a clear pattern of feedback around his decision making style, helping him understand the cost, and how other leaders shared decision power. Like in

Charles Dickens' <u>A Christmas Carol</u>, seeing ourselves through the eyes of others can be a powerful way to increase motivation to change.

4. Amp up the ability; will often follows skill

This strategy seems a bit odd until you realize that the skill often comes before the will. Does a 9-year old want to learn to play the piano? Yet once they get traction and can play a song, the desire to play often increases.

The challenge with this approach is getting them to invest in skill building enough that eventually it results in increased motivation. So if parents, bosses, or friends can spend some of their influence capital in getting an agreement to *some* training, that may be enough to tip the scales of motivation.

Lockheed Martin used managers to teach a class on direct communication. Many managers weren't all that interested in teaching, yet when asked, they reluctantly agreed. Few anticipated the passion for the topic that soon became obvious as they began to improve their own abilities for respectfully candid accountability conversations. What got them excited about the topic? Increased skill building increased their motivation as they saw tangible results.

Summary

We all know that you can lead a horse to water but you can't make him drink. But you can link the water to what he most wants if you know him well enough. You can use feedback and consequences to help him see the value of drinking, or increase his drinking skill which often results in increased motivation.

Now that you have insights for dealing with low motivation, our final stop is navigating the accountability conversation that has gone sideways.

Chapter Ten: Getting a Disaster Back on Track

The union negotiations had bogged down to the point of being pointless. Years of power plays had taken their toll and it clouded the options on both sides of the table. A strike seemed unavoidable.

The consultant suggested that both sides step back and talk about the health of the relationship rather than butting heads on the issues. They agreed out of despair.

This was fruitful. Both sides acknowledged past sins, identified areas of mutual interest, the consequences of a poor relationship, and began the steps of rebuilding trust. There was no magic other than an acknowledgment that they shared a common fate and it was in everyone's best interest to keep the lines of communication open as they worked on the relationship.

This same dynamic plays out in all accountability conversations. If we're focusing at the wrong level, we'll see no real progress unless we shift the conversation to address the real need.

Accountability conversations live on three levels: events, patterns, and relationships.

Event

Level one is the issue, event or what's happening now.

Pattern

Level two is a pattern or events or issues over time, where events are much less relevant than the pattern of actions over time.

Relationship

Level three addresses the foundation of the relationship. When the relationship struggles with low trust and past baggage, conversations at Levels 1 and 2 aren't productive. When trust is at risk, nothing else matters.

So the first skill in dealing with a derailed accountability conversation is to understand what level needs to be dealt with and focused on. No other fix will work when you're simply focusing at the wrong level.

A manager wanted to turn around the performance of a key employee who had once been a superstar. Yet accountability conversations seemed to be falling flat.

67

At first the conversations focused on dropped balls or events (level 1), but there seemed to be something lacking in the follow through in spite of clear commitments. Then the manager shifted to patterns or level 2 since the issues continued. The employee seemed to understand more of what he needed to change in order to get his performance back on track. Pattern-level conversations helped highlight the need to change but again, the behavior shifted back.

I asked the manager if he trusted the employee. Of course he didn't. So we decided it was time to talk to a deeper level, where relationship dynamics and trust are the focus and goal.

When the manager framed the goal to increase trust so he could once again rely on him as a top performer, improvement accelerated. Events and even patterns paled in comparison to the real issue of broken trust.

In all accountability conversations, look first at trust and the relationship level to see if the conversation needs to focus there. When trust is at risk, nothing else matters. That must become the goal or topic, rather than an event. The exception is when we don't have an ongoing relationship yet need to address an issue.

Next, if there is a pattern of bad behavior, work at that level rather than focusing only on one event. Don't argue an event when there is a clear pattern that needs to be changed.

Redo the Opening, Then Assess the Level

I got a strong response once from a guy I thought would welcome the conversation. I opened well, really respected this guy, and he came back with anger.

How would you respond? I smiled and started again. I've found that empathy followed by opening again helps the conversation.

"You sound angry. I don't want to suggest disrespect or a lack of appreciation of your abilities. I do want to talk about how we can work together more effectively so we avoid duplication. Are you open to that?"

He quieted down once he saw that I wasn't getting upset and my goal was to talk through improved coordination. Acknowledging his emotion plus restating my goal seemed to help. That kept the door open to explore the issue further.

As we discussed our working relationship, it became clear to me that we needed to drop down to the relationship level and talk about trust and some assumptions he had about me. You can guess that he heard some things about me that led him to believe I didn't like him, trust him,

69

and that I wanted his job. None of these things were true and he believed my explanations. Soon the fog lifted and we could talk about more concrete actions to align our work.

An easy accountability conversation turned into an emotional reaction that became a relationship intervention, but nothing else would have set us on a new path. What worked was keeping calm, knowing what I wanted out of the conversation, dealing with this outburst and then seeing that we needed to go deeper into more fundamental relationship issues.

We both noticed productivity, a more enjoyable working relationship, and I experienced more joy at work. One good conversation brought good results. But I also felt a sense of accomplishment every time I worked with this guy. The disaster turned out to be just the catalyst we needed to break through to new levels of performance.

Every difficult conversation, every conflict carries the seed of opportunity, to solve a problem and move relationships to new levels of trust.

Can that be true of the accountability conversations we have with our boss? Let's find out in the next chapter.

Chapter Eleven: Boss Accountability Conversations

I don't believe in confronting people but in helping them act in their own best interest as I pursue mine. I say this because, often when someone discovers the power of speaking up, they come to enjoy the confrontation, the power of speaking truth, yet lose the breakthrough opportunity that comes from advancing the needs and goals of others while meeting your own.

Enter the boss. If you work in a large organization, you have many bosses. I've been one and have coached many others. They're people who have emotional needs and are pursuing goals. Read: they are people.

Yet these people wield a great deal of influence in the organization and over your career. No wonder we hold back in sharing the truth about failing projects, feedback on their behavior, our failures, because doing so has proven to be risky.

I supported a project that was heading for a cliff. Everyone knew it except our executive sponsors. They had invested dollars, resources, and put

71

their own reputations on the line for the project. And they drove the team with an iron fist. Failure was not an option.

But testing showed poor software design that would require more training to navigate a poor user interface. No one believed we would hit the launch date. Testers kept telling users that their frustrations would be fixed before system launch even though they knew it wouldn't. Yet each time we started to share the risks, they pushed back lectures on making it happen.

Cynicism stalked the halls around the project team. People were quietly trying to find the exit. I figured I had nothing to lose in having an accountability conversation with one key leader who seemed the most resistant to reality in our sponsor reviews. It was one on one time.

In my golden minute, I thought about my own emotions, conclusions and got myself into a calm, rational, and clear place of understanding what I wanted and what I believed he wanted. I opened the conversation talking about the goal of project success; what I was seeing and hearing at the project level, ask him how open he was to the conversation.

In I dove.

"Ray, I know we both are committed to project success and I'm seeing some things I want to discuss, not to complain, but to talk about what might derail us and how to manage our risk. That includes some things I'm seeing at your level. How open are you to exploring this?"

He nodded like he had heard this five times that morning. Good start I thought. Then it occurred to me. I was giving feedback in service of a goal he cared about. This wasn't complaining or criticizing, but a useful view that big boys share with other big boys so they land the goals they care about. Mutual purpose and a tone of respect created the desire to dig in.

I shared the team view, some dynamics that clearly hurt our effectiveness. He nodded, and then said, "You said I was part of the problem? That's something I need to hear."

Gulp. I brought myself back to calm.

Surprisingly he admitted he too felt the project wasn't on track and to my delight, owned his role in the problem. Encouraged, I shared more of what I was seeing, what I believed was the plan to get it back on track, and what we needed from him. We created a plan and immediately started to implement fixes. Some key leaders were replaced as we retooled and shifted our implementation schedule. An effective conversation saved a project failure.

Accountability conversations save money and drive results. Making them a habit creates a culture, a pattern of behavior that saves money and accelerates results.

But what was the cost of waiting to speak up? I wonder the same thing as I hear employees complaining about situations they know are not right, yet don't speak up. I am convinced that one good accountability conversation can turn many of these situations around. As I said before, every conversation carries the seed of opportunity, for breakthrough in problems and relationships.

Special Considerations for Bosses

By far the biggest perception gap with leaders is that they believe they are open to feedback but in fact dread it. A friend who administers 360 feedback surveys to thousands of executives said that few people are truly open to and value feedback while most see themselves as very open to it.

Yet I've also found that leaders are highly-motivated, goal seeking individuals. Yes they need respect, to be understood, but I've found that once I understand their level of desire towards a goal, I can provide feedback to that level.

Think of it like a gate. The size and width of the gate is their desire to attain a goal. Small gate = limited feedback; large window = abundant feedback.

Identify Goals and Values

Therefore, find out what they care about. Then you can temper your accountability conversation to their level of goal attainment desire.

How do you find out? Ask and listen. I ask questions about the future they want to see personally, professionally, and organizationally. I find out how they spend their discretionary time. I listen to their success stories for clues about their values, what they avoid the most and most want. I ask those who know them these questions, what they tend to avoid and what tends to motivate them. I do so because that information will temper what goals I link to in my accountability conversations and how direct I can be in sharing observations, patterns, or in dealing with relationship-level issues.

Once I think I've found a good goal or value to link to, I try it out in an accountability conversation to see how they respond.

Example

Rick is a seasoned executive who runs IT for a large software development organization. From conversations I've had with those who know him, he's highly motivated to find favor with his senior Officer team, avoid embarrassment, and leave a legacy for the organization. He wants to make a name for himself in an organization of high achievers.

And he wants to change his culture to be more respectfully candid and instill the value of cooperation, getting people out of their silos to align more to business goals. I have an opening to discuss some obvious issues of poor coordination and alignment on his team. In short, two members of his team take every opportunity to undermine each other and he chooses not to take action.

He knows me as I've worked with their leadership team on Talent Management issues in the past. I open the conversation with "Rick, thanks for meeting with me. I'll be working with your team on shifting the culture to cooperate more and be more respectfully candid. I want to share some early observations of what's working and what's not, get your feedback and reactions, and discuss some possible next steps. How does that sound?"

He's open. He wants more cooperation and candor. And, we haven't discussed the more personal side that he's part of the problem.

After sharing some instances of poor coordination, and alignment on his team, I say, "I don't want to make you feel defensive, but how do you see your role in what's going on?" He pauses, raises his eye brows, takes a deep breath and we both endure a long silence. I wait.

"I've been hoping that these guys fix their own problems but it's probably time for dad to break up the fight. Is that what you were hoping to hear?"

I reinforce my goal and I hope it's his goal as well. Keeping the conversation linked to a goal they care about keeps the lines of communication open.

"I'm here to raise insights into what will move IT to the next level of cooperation and candor." He nods in agreement. It seems that my goal is his goal.

As we move to analysis and commitment, he wants our conversation to be replayed with his team so they all have an opportunity to own their part of the problem, explore solutions, and make commitments. And that started a series of conversations that made this organization better. It started with his desire to improve, shifted forward with a good accountability conversation that led to a series of candid conversations that changed behavior.

What made this moment possible? I started with me, respected him, and was clear on my goal and his goal. I stated my observations, my data points, tried to stay away from accusation or conclusions, and asked many questions. I kept the conversation anchored to the mutual goal so the candor felt meaningful rather than an exercise in criticism.

Summary

Accountability conversations with the power brokers of an organization are like any other because people are people. Yet attention to the golden moment, sharing feedback in service of a goal they care about, careful analysis and clear commitments change behavior when it matters most.

Your confidence in these moments comes from a strong golden minute that includes acknowledgment of your emotions, conclusions, what you want, what they want, and staying anchored to that. When your conversation is about helping them get what they want, the difficult conversation becomes much easier.

Chapter Twelve: From Poor Confrontation to Results

My jaw dropped as I listened to a team member rant to me. Accusations like "you're undermining this team with your arrogant and isolated decisions" stunned me. I don't see myself like that. Yet he held that conclusion as truth and shared in a forceful, unproductive way.

How can you help others help you even when they do so poorly, creating defensiveness and an unproductive conversation environment?

I know from experience that if you match their toxic emotions, giving them back what they're dishing out, up go the walls nothing good will come out of this.

What does work when someone attacks you? Five key behaviors will turn any unproductive conversation into one that can change behavior for the good.

1. Acknowledge the emotions of the person coming at you

2. Seek a common goal or purpose

3. Move away from conclusions to understand what was done, observed, or said

4. Set strong conversation boundaries

5. Create clear commitments

You know by now that all good crisis intervention counselors meet strong emotions with acknowledgment and by redirecting the emotional energy to a common goal.

Here is an example of a good response to an emotional outburst that amounted to a character smear at a team off-site day. Tom was frustrated and said, "You're the problem. We seemed fine until you joined the team."

Stunned, I sprang into action to see if I could turn this to a productive conversation.

"Tom, you sound upset and this sounds like strong feedback. I want us to talk through this so you feel heard, but I need to understand what's causing you to say this so, if need be, I can adjust what I'm doing. How does that sound?"

He was calming. He nodded in agreement. I suspected his anger was more about other frustrations but I was open to any insights that would help me perform better. I used a calm but firm voice. I didn't match is emotional intensity but modeled what I wanted from him. *Calm.*

I added a boundary and a personal acknowledgment.

"Tom, I'm feeling defensive right now and I know that's not helpful. So what I need from you is more of what you're observing rather than these general statements. Walk me into what led you to see me this way."

He shared a story, not observations. He said, "When you joined this team, you thought you knew everything, that we were just a bunch of hicks. We're respected in this organization and it's time you started respecting us."

He's clearly operating in a belief but I needed to get him to share the data, the observations, and the events that created this belief. He ignored my previous question so I tried again.

"Tom, I understand you believe this, but I'm struggling to see what led you to believe this. I do respect this team and I respect you, but what specifically have you seen that's leading you to believe I don't respect you or the team."

He started sharing expectation violations I considered to be minor. I'm a task guy and he was relationship oriented. I came in and got right to work rather than socializing. To him that meant I was arrogant while in my head, I was simply trying to maximize the precious resource of time.

When I became the team leader, I held team meetings less frequently because we didn't need them. Again, he interpreted my actions in the worse possible way. Added to that, he saved all his toxic conclusions for the outburst I was attempting to navigate.

The conversation shifted when I did a quick golden moment, got calm again, and started the accountability conversation again.

"Tom, I didn't mean any disrespect by canceling team meetings. It's my style to focus on tasks, which may be seen as my being unconcerned for others. That's not my intent. I want us to talk about how we can get back on the same page. How does that sound?"

I started asking questions to understand more, what actions communicated respect for him. Soon I began to understand how he saw life. It was all about the little things, the informal conversation, the lunch meetings, questions about his family, all the things I simply didn't have time for because I was carrying the workload for an underperforming team.

We needed more accountability conversations to dig deeper, to talk about my views of how the team was underperforming, his role it in, and what we could do differently. I became more sociable and he became more task oriented.

Good came from a bad confrontation turned into a productive accountability conversation. It can start bad but don't let it end that way. You have the insight and skills to turn awkward or unproductive conversations into something that positively affects behavior.

Summary

When other people come at you in unproductive ways, seek to move it back on track by doing the following:

1. Acknowledge the emotions of the person coming at you

2. Seek a common goal or purpose

3. Move away from conclusions to understand what was done, observed, or said

4. Set strong conversation boundaries

5. Create clear commitments

Create the habit by imaging that someone is coming at you with accusation, then seeing yourself deal with this productively and feeling the payoff.

Appendix A: Frequently Asked Questions

These questions come from years of coaching and training experience in this topic. These represent the most common and compelling questions that enrich learning and insight in this critical skill.

I did the golden minute but it was an awkward conversation as others were listening in and that seemed to add pressure we didn't need. Thoughts?

Yes, take people aside to have a private conversation. I thought I could do a quick accountability conversation with an employee in a cubicle environment only to find there was more that needed to be discussed. It didn't go well with others listening in. I shut down the conversation and moved it into a private conference room. Yes, keep accountability conversations private.

Why didn't you start with commitment making in your model? Because isn't that the first step, to make sure they know what we expect?

85

I put the most important information up-front, the golden minute, because mastery there translates into the most productive outcomes.

And I've found that even with great expectation setting, we always find breakdowns that need to be addressed. We find out the unwritten rules of any new group by violating them. Good accountability conversations help everyone by knowing how to adjust behavior and by building the relationship because we deal with gaps respectfully.

Does it matter about a past relationship history when we are talking to someone, confronting them?

In chapter 10 I shared the levels of conversation that included event, pattern, and relationship. Relationship-level conversations get at the deep issues but I've also found that small wins with small issues build momentum. Success builds trust, trust you'll need to tackle the bigger, deeper issues.

How does this book compare with Crucial Confrontations and Fierce Conversations? Which is best?

The two books you mention are excellent. Both recognize the need for effective conversation skills when commitments are not met or we see bad behavior. We emphasize habit formation, the golden minute, especially the part that deals with emotional intelligence. We've found that a focus on creating the habit associated with the golden minute makes these conversations more likely and higher quality. We also provide analysis and commitment conversation tools that many find helpful.

Every time I speak up to my boss, I get shot down. I try to be respectful and link my feedback to his goals, but he seems defensive. Suggestions?

What are you thinking when you open the conversation? I learned the hard way many years ago that what I'm thinking does come through to the other person. Honestly examine whether the problem may be your preparation and not his character.

When I hit a wall like this, I like to ask the other person how to raise issues in a way that addresses issues but doesn't produce defensiveness. I ask them who does that well, what they do, and what I need to learn to better help them create results. Often that opens the door to helpful insights and feedback I in turn use when offering feedback.

One other side benefit of doing this is that most bosses respect those who speak up productively. They don't respect victims who complain behind their back or people who overreact.

I tried the habit exercises you describe but still find I avoid these conversations. It's just not a habit. What can I do?

When a habit isn't "taking," it's often an issue of how we view difficult conversations. We avoid pain naturally, so unless we change to a belief that opportunity is found in each accountability conversation, we will avoid them.

Identify situations in as much detail that would trigger the golden minute. Write it down in the far left hand column of a 4 column sheet. See below.

Then identify your first emotional reaction in the next to the left column.

Then write down exactly what you will do in this situation. Be as specific as you can. Write it down.

Then in the far right column, identify the emotional payoff for speaking up in a productive way.

Situation	Initial	My Actions	Emotional

	Reaction		Payoff

As you analyze your triggers and your response, consider the beliefs and expectations that guide your behavior. Is there opportunity to change behavior and build a relationship or do you believe that speaking up brings nothing but pain? You beliefs shape your expectations which in turn shape your behavior.

As you challenge your beliefs and have better experiences, you will soon come to enjoy new results regularly. That's the power of habit; you'll have a new habitual response that serves you well. And you'll wonder why you ever avoided difficult conversations to begin with.